Speak Over the Fear

DR. STEPHANIE L. FOSTER

Speak Over the Fear

Copyright ©2019 Dr. Stephanie L. Foster

Library of Congress Control Number 2019941609

All rights reserved. No part of this book may be used or reproduced in any manner whatsoever without written permission from the publisher and copyright holder, except for the inclusion of brief quotations in a review.

The information presented in this book is based on the author's research and experience. Every attempt has been made to ensure the presented information is accurate; however, the author cannot accept liability for any errors that may exist. The reader assumes all responsibility for the consequences of actions taken based on information presented in this book.

Unless otherwise noted, Scripture quotations are taken from the Holy Bible, New International Version®, NIV®. Copyright©1973, 1978, 1984, 2011 by Biblica, Inc.™ Used by permission of Zondervan. All rights reserved worldwide. www.zondervan.com. The "NIV" and "New International Version" are trademarks registered in the United States Patent and Trademark Office by Biblica, Inc.™

Published by Intentionally Me, LLC
comms@intentionallymellc.com

Interior Design | Cover Design
DHBonner Virtual Solutions LLC
www.dhbonner.net

ISBN (print): 978-1-7330162-0-9
ISBN (e-book): 978-1-7330162-1-6

Published in the United States of America

DEDICATION

This book is for Believers who are dreamers and doers, determined to fulfill their life purposes. I share your determination.

I believe God is pleased with our determination to use our God-given talents to demonstrate His goodness and love.

God is our ever-present Help, calling and empowering us to be overcomers and more than conquerors (Psalm 46:1, 1 John 5:4, and Romans 8:37).

God is *The Omniscient, Omnipresent, and Omnipotent One*. He is with and for us. God's plans for our lives are good (Jeremiah 29:11). We are God's masterpieces, created to do good works (Ephesians 2:10).

God is love (1 John 4:16). God loves each of us unconditionally (Jeremiah 31:3 and John 3:16-17).

As we mature and trust God's love for us, love will displace fear (1 John 4:18). Love and fear can't occupy the same space.

Love doesn't quit or give up (1 Corinthians 13:7).

We won't quit or give up. We are overcomers and more than conquerors!

Table of Contents

INTRODUCTION 1

PART ONE: MINDSET 5

    I Matter!.. 5

    Someone Needs Me to Be Me! 6

    I Speak What I Believe!.. 7

PART TWO: LANGUAGE 10

    No! 11

    Yes! 12

    I Want.. 14

    I Need.. 18

    I Will... 19

    I Choose... 21

    I Am.. 23

    I Believe in My Dreams! 26

    I Can! 27

PART THREE: BEHAVIORS 31

    Dream Big! 31

    Plan How You Can 34

    Show Up! 35

Take Your Place! 36
Take a Step Forward Every Day! 41

CLOSING 45
ABOUT THE AUTHOR 50
REFERENCES 51

Introduction

I rushed to the car, leaving Mom in the theater to joke with other parents whose kids had tried out for *The Wiz*. I had nothing to laugh about. For days, I had begged her to take me to the try out. Once there, I recognized the director and kids from my high school's acclaimed theater group. When called to the stage, the kids chirped, pranced, and emoted liked professionals while the director beamed and clapped with approval.

My hands began to sweat, my stomach churned, and my mind screamed, *"What were you thinking? You can't compete with these kids! Save your pride, pretend you're here to support the kids from your school, and leave as quickly as you can without drawing attention!"*

My turn to walk onstage and sing came. The stage challenged me: *You do know that everyone will see and hear every mistake you make! Come on up! You've only got your dignity to lose.* I swiftly responded. I gripped my seat, refused to let go, and ignored Mom's indignation.

Decades later, I am pleased my wounds from previous speaking refusals have healed. The remaining scars and lessons learned are compelling proof of an authentic life – a unique combination of goodness and vulnerability.

Have you, like me, ever allowed fear to stop you? If so, you were agreeing with fear. Fear is skilled in keeping you small and contained, convincing you all the while that staying small is for your benefit. Fear lulls you into believing the familiar is fine. "Sure," fear chants, "just go along to get along" or "it is what it is." Proof of these mindsets includes just living for the weekend and/or participating in other activities that fill your waking hours, yet numb your soul. If you're content with that kind of living, this book isn't for you.

This book is for the person who wants to leave the self-imposed cage of self-denial and rush into the wide expanse of possibility – free to pursue and live a purposeful life. If that's you, this book is for you. Know you're not alone in this journey. I am with you, as are countless others. I'll gladly share some of my past and ongoing experiences in learning how to *Speak Over the Fear*. Relax and have no fear (*yes, the pun is intentional*). All is, and will be, well.

To orient you, the book has three parts to correlate with two of our three dimensions as human beings. Going from the inside out, we are spirit beings, possessing souls, and living in physical bodies. As Believers, our spirit beings have been recreated to align with God. It's our souls (minds, wills, and emotions) and bodies that have to be renewed to God's way of thinking and being. Accordingly, Part One focuses on mindset; Part Two focuses on language; and Part Three focuses on behaviors.

The book's title, *Speak Over the Fear*, addresses our authority as spirit beings. Genesis 1:27 shares how God created human beings in His image. God is a word-speaking spirit being who uses language for creative purposes and governance. Made in God's image, God gave human beings the ability to speak words that carry authority. Proverbs 18:21 cautions that words produce life or death and the speaker will live with the consequences of his/her words. You could think of words as buckets that will contain whatever water you pour in them. If you pour in fresh, clean water, you will reap health benefits from drinking the fresh, clean water. If you pour in polluted, contaminated water, you will reap a harvest of toxins capable of causing damage and destruction. You will reap what you sow. In Deuteronomy 30:19, God counsels us, "This day I call the heavens and the earth as witnesses against you that I have set before you life and death, blessings and curses. Now choose life, so that you and your children may live."

To *Speak Over the Fear* is to choose life and speak what God says about you in the face of fear and other circumstances that would attempt to dominate and victimize you. To *Speak Over the Fear* is to boldly apply 2 Corinthians 10:5, which directs us to "…demolish arguments and every pretension that sets itself up against the knowledge of God, and we take captive every thought to make it obedient to Christ."

Please reread the dedication. Really, read it again. Throughout the Bible, God speaks of His love, design, and empowerment of us. God, *The Omniscient, Omnipresent, and Omnipotent One*, asserts we are beloved, His masterpieces, overcomers, and more than conquerors.

Overcomers and conquerors are made in the training grounds of obscurity and revealed in public demonstrations of matured faith and action. Wherever you are in your faith journey and whatever your challenges, take heart. God, *The Omniscient, Omnipresent, and Omnipotent One*, says, "Be strong and courageous. Do not be afraid or terrified because of them, for the LORD your God goes with you; he will never leave you nor forsake you" (Deuteronomy 31:6).

Faith is **now** (Hebrews 11:1). **Now** is our time to act. **Now** is the time to speak life (God's Word) over our circumstances. **Now** is the time to embrace the mindsets, language, and behaviors to *Speak Over the Fear*. Victory is so near, as close as our mouths and hearts (Romans 10:8).

What are we waiting for? ***Let's get started!***

PART ONE: MINDSET

I Matter!

Generally, a chair is for sitting and a lamp is for light. Both items are designed to meet specific needs. Their presence matters. If you think otherwise, consider a house lacking these items. Would you want to live there?

How about you? What is your purpose? How are you an answer to needs within our world? Just as manufacturers design chairs and lamps to meet specific needs, we are God's workmanship (Ephesians 2:10). God created us for specific purposes. If we are out of place, important needs will be unmet and people – known and unknown to us – will suffer. A classic example of this is Abraham Lincoln, the 16th President of the United States. Various disappointments, losses, and defeats marked his life journey. These setbacks provided compelling reasons to give up on his aspirations before and during his presidency.

Ever resilient, his actions in securing passage of the 13th Amendment transformed our nation's history and generations of lives. One life matters.

One life matters. Each life matters. Individually and collectively, we have assignments to fulfill.

Someone Needs Me to Be Me!

It is easy to put off until tomorrow what can be done today. Why do we think things will be easier tomorrow? My experience has shown the opposite. Procrastination is a thief, robbing you of valuable time. Though certain seasons of our lives seem like they will never end, we only have a short amount of time to work.

If your work only impacted you, the consequences of procrastination and inaction would be minimized, but that's not the case. God has created you with talents others need.

If fear and/or self-limiting beliefs are keeping you from doing what you know you should do, I recommend you consider two things:

1. God decided your purpose before designing your being. You are designed to fulfill your purpose! You are designed to succeed at being you!
2. There are people and achievements waiting for you on the other side of fear and self-limiting beliefs.

Returning to Abraham Lincoln's example, I'm glad he didn't do what was politically convenient. My life experiences and aspirations are possible today because of his life decisions made more than a century before my birth. Every time I watch the movie *Lincoln,* I am moved to tears by Lincoln's resolve to act on behalf of millions of people yet to be born. I am grateful.

I Speak What I Believe!

If I believe I matter and someone needs me to be me, it is and should be difficult for me to hoard my talents for self-gain or hide my talents out of misguided self-deprecation. Why? Because I know the value of who I am and what I can do.

Beliefs shape and permeate actions. I think of beliefs as roots, often invisible beneath the ground. Conversely, fruits are typically highly visible above ground. Roots feed fruits. Similarly, beliefs feed actions. If I want to understand my actions, I need to analyze my beliefs. This can be uncomfortable if my actions are self-destructive. Actions speak. Actions also show what I believe. Whether I like it or not, my actions speak what I believe.

Knowing this, I choose to embrace beliefs that bring out the best in me. This power of choice is my birthright. You have the same power to choose what you believe about yourself. Fear knows this. Fear will go to extreme lengths to make you think you're powerless. Fear will readily use other people, circumstances, and even your own thoughts to contain you. Ever the bully, fear will taunt, strut, and denounce your efforts. Fear will also strive to get you to doubt God's love and good plans for you. Returning to the Introduction's bucket example, fear is a contaminant.

If you remain silent because of or agree with fear, you will reap a harvest of fear-dominated results. But if you choose to respond with God's Word and dare to believe in the value of who you are and what you can do as God's child, you can defeat fear – every time and with every action that positions God's power to work on your behalf.

Hmm, now would be a perfect time to reacquaint yourself with David's defeat of Goliath. Chapter 17 of 1 Samuel records how the taunts of **one** giant Philistine warrior frightened King Saul's **entire** army. How was David, a young shepherd, able to defeat Goliath, an experienced champion warrior? What can you learn from David's example in confronting Goliath? Getting more personal, what Goliaths are taunting you? *More importantly, what words of God are you speaking over these taunts?*

God can do what He promises (Romans 4:21). People get what God promises by having faith in Him (Romans 4:16). Abraham's journey to fatherhood as recorded in Romans 4:18 was profound: "Against all hope, Abraham in hope believed and so became the father of many nations, just as it had been said to him, 'So shall your offspring be.'"

Challenges are part of life. What are you speaking in response to your life challenges?

Points to Remember

1. We are God's workmanship (Ephesians 2:10), created for specific purposes. If we are out of place, important needs will be unmet and people – known and unknown to us – will suffer.
2. God has created you with talents others need.
3. You are designed to fulfill your purpose!
4. Fear will go to extreme lengths to make you think you're powerless.
5. If you choose to respond with God's Word and dare to believe in the value of who you are and what you can do as God's child, you can defeat fear – every time and with every action that positions God's power to work on your behalf.

PART TWO: LANGUAGE

Words are elements of language. The words we speak are gatekeepers of our use of time, maintenance of relationships, and pursuit of goals.

Our words have the power to provide a perimeter defense to safeguard what matters to us. Our words also have the power to launch insider attacks against ourselves. How vigilant are you in monitoring your internal dialogue?

In 2017, I had to challenge my resistance to boldly acting on my own behalf. That year, I did something I should have done years earlier: I nominated myself for a TEDx event and it was much easier than I had imagined.

When I first saw information about a local 2017 TEDx event, I got excited but almost immediately heard myself say, "*Why should you be selected? Who will nominate you?*" The nomination form loomed in front of me. Yes, I knew I could ask others to nominate me, but I also knew I'd probably have to prepare the nomination and monitor their actions – hopefully without getting on their nerves – to ensure they submitted the nomination on time. From deep within, a bold thought raced across my mind: "*How about nominating myself? Why not?*"

I could list other opportunities when I should have nominated myself and didn't. Each time, I had ignored an unction to act. I had reasoned that if I deserved such an opportunity, others would validate and act on my behalf. I was wrong.

In 2017, I changed my mind. I sat down, ignored my doubts, and acted. Instead of one, I submitted *several* TEDx self-nominations. I said "*Yes!*" to myself, my dreams, and my future. And I'll do it again and again!

My journey to self-nomination can be traced by the words I spoke to myself. In moving from the position of believing others should validate my dreams to occupying the position of boldly acting on my own behalf, the words "*No!*" and "*Yes!*" and "*I want…*" became my enablers.

NO!

No is a complete sentence. *No* is a complete thought. *No* doesn't need explanation, excuses, or external permission. *No* doesn't mean maybe or possibly. *No* means "*No!*"

In my journey to self-nomination, my shift began with my decision to say *"No!"* to wasting desired opportunities because others weren't advocating on my behalf. My priorities aren't necessarily others' priorities, especially if I haven't taken decisive action to express these goals to others. In my experience, solely wishing is an insufficient and unrewarding strategy.

Practice saying "No!"

Think about recent situations when you've wanted to say *"No!"* but didn't. Think about why you didn't say *"No!"* and what you'd do differently if you had a do-over. Think forward to tomorrow and think of a likely situation in which you want to say *"No!"* Take ten minutes to envision and practice saying *"No!"* to this situation.

If saying *"No!"* seems challenging, reflect on toddlers who readily and unapologetically assert *"No!"* They aren't disowned for their statements and neither should you be. Remember what's important to you and choose to be deliberate and skilled in saying *"No!"* as needed.

YES!

Give yourself permission to be and do. *Yes* is the master password, enabling entry of desired life experiences. Decide what you desire to become and own this decision. Say "*Yes!*" to the thoughts and actions needed to reach your goals.

The mere contemplation of self-nomination was revolutionary to me. Instead of waiting for someone else to determine my qualification, self-nomination asserted *I deemed myself qualified.* I was the first to say, "*Yes!*" to my attainment of a desired life experience. Wow – what a sense of empowerment!

Practice saying "Yes!":

Think about recent situations when you yearned to say "*Yes!*" but didn't. Think about why you didn't say "*Yes!*" and what you'd do differently if you had a do-over. Think forward to tomorrow and think of a likely situation in which you need to say "*Yes!*" Take ten minutes to envision and practice saying "*Yes!*" to this situation.

If saying "*Yes!*" seems challenging, reflect on trailblazers and role models who defy the status quo and unapologetically assert "*Yes!*" to their dreams. Unfazed by others' doubts and rejection, they proceed. Regardless of the outcome of their dreams' pursuit, these trailblazers stand as testaments of the audacity of dreamers. Who would you rather stand with — dreamers, critics, or bystanders? You have one life to live and the magnitude of your life's heights are shaped by your willingness to say "*Yes!*" to the possibility of your dreams.

I WANT…

Identify what you want and speak it out loud…to yourself and others. Unapologetically acknowledge what matters to you. I wanted to be a TEDx speaker. The selection process begins with a speaker nomination. Speaker self-nominations are accepted. *I could take the action needed to launch my dream.* I wanted to be a TEDx speaker, so I submitted self-nominations to multiple events.

Practice saying *"I want…"*:

Think of recent situations when you wanted to speak up and say, *"I want…"*, but didn't. How did you feel? When I do this, I typically feel the rise of resentment towards myself and the situation. *Why did I let [fill in the blank] do this again and why didn't I say what I really want?* If this resonates with you, the good news is that when other opportunities arise to speak your preferences, you can be prepared to do so!

Preparation empowers! Like you did in the previous practice sessions for saying *"No!"* and *"Yes!"*, think about why you didn't say *"I want…"* and what you'd do differently if you had a do-over. Think forward to tomorrow and think of a likely situation in which you need to say *"I want…"*. Take ten minutes to envision and practice saying *"I want…"* to this situation.

Build up this speaking muscle by practicing basic situations. Consider tomorrow's lunch. Presuming you want to eat a lunch that's healthy and provides the nourishment you need for the next hours' work, make the best decision from your options. Skipping lunch is a typical option, yet it counters your want for healthy nourishment and stamina. So, have a plan in place to overcome the temptation to skip lunch. Whether you bring or buy your lunch, be consistent in eating a healthy lunch. Others may deride your actions, but your future self will thank you.

You have one life to live. Use wisdom and discernment in safeguarding your priorities and wants. If you're going to skip anything, starve your fears and feed your faith.

We are all works in progress. Diving deeper into our study of words as a perimeter defense to safeguard what matters to us, I will now reflect on earlier lessons gained in using my will to pursue my needs.

One experience that readily comes to mind is my journey to getting braces as an adult. I'm naturally a smiler, but my smile hasn't always been a source of joy. In my teens, my incisors protruded awkwardly, giving my smile a crowded appearance. My family didn't say much about my teeth, but it troubled me to have a problem everyone could see, and I couldn't fix.

Why didn't I get braces? I don't know. I don't remember seeing other kids with braces…it just seemed to be something I had to live with. During frequent moves as part of military family life, my crowded teeth and waning smile didn't make the top ten list of concerns. My job was to be a good kid, excel in school, and get into a good college. My teeth didn't interfere with these things, so I soldiered on.

As my college classmates began to marry and start families, I became more uncomfortable with my smile. Were crowded teeth scaring off my Mr. Right? With much trepidation, I asked a married mentor whose teeth mirrored mine about what to do. "Girl, you're smart and nice — don't worry about it. Look at me! I've got the same thing and I'm okay — I've got a wife." Yes, he had a beautiful wife and family. I tried to embrace his words, but all I could see were his incisors protruding from his gums, dancing with defiance as he mouthed platitudes.

He was okay with crooked teeth, but I was not. I wanted more and better for myself! In that moment and with that thought, I decided I would get braces — no matter what!

Crooked teeth didn't bother my mentor, but they bothered me. As I considered my situation, my mind and spirit battled. Spirit urged me to do what I needed to have my smile match my personality and outlook on life. Mind questioned the cost, pain, and need to fix something that really wasn't broken — after all, I was doing well and *"if a guy doesn't like you because of your smile, he obviously isn't the right guy for you."*

Thinking harder, I grappled with my beliefs. I knew my smile represented more than an aesthetic feature to attract others. My smile was my outer witness of my sense of wellbeing. For me, the very act of smiling is freedom of choice. No matter what may be going on around me, I can choose to smile broadly, knowing that somehow, I'd be okay.

In choosing to be peaceful, I'd snatch the oxygen from the fires of toxic thoughts trying to overwhelm me...toxic thoughts doubting my lovability, worth, ability, etc. However, in being so self-conscious of my smile, I was losing my confidence like a balloon slowly deflating. Saddest of all, I was doing this to myself.

Quickly, I realized I was the key to this matter. **If my inaction was causing my increasing discomfort, then surely my action could turn the situation around.** In that moment and with that thought, I decided I would get braces — no matter what!

I NEED…

Identify what you need and speak it out loud…to yourself and others. It's also okay to ask for help. Being able to assess your needs and get what you need, positions you to achieve what you desire.

Life is challenging enough without the added burden of being uncomfortable in your own skin. For me, crooked teeth presented chaos I didn't feel or want in my life. This discrepancy taunted my desire for peace within and without. Knowing my need for peace, I began my search for help. As a cadet and 2nd Lieutenant, I pursued free orthodontic care. Interestingly, my condition didn't meet treatment criteria and I found myself as a brand new 2nd Lieutenant with an undesirable, yet fixable condition.

"Lead, follow, or get out of the way!" was the title and message of my first speech as a 2nd Lieutenant. I truly believed what I said to members of my battalion. I felt good about the message until I noticed I had begun to cover my mouth while smiling.

Startled, I looked at my hands. The same hands that covered my smile could be the same hands to set my smile free. My crooked teeth were fixable. Instead of being a victim of a bureaucratic decision, I could rise and be part of the solution. I could lead myself to my desired future of a beautiful set of straight teeth.

Practice saying *"I need..."*:

Think about recent situations when you've wanted to say *"I need..."* but didn't. Think about why you didn't say *"I need..."* and what you'd do differently if you had a do-over. Think forward to tomorrow and think of a likely situation in which you want to say, *"I need...."* Take ten minutes to envision and practice saying *"I need..."* to this situation.

Think about the benefits you'll experience from getting what you need. Reach for these benefits and choose to be deliberate and skilled in saying *"I need..."* as often as needed.

I WILL...

Engage your will in standing up for yourself. Back to my story, my crooked teeth were fixable. Since my wearing of braces wouldn't impede my duty performance, my chain of command had no objection to me getting braces. Various civilian orthodontists were located near my German base. I just needed to solve the problem of payment.

I was a single 2nd Lieutenant living in the Bachelor's Officer Quarters (*translation: I was a young, unmarried professional with minimal living expenses*). Could I pay for the braces? Absolutely! Yes, I could pay for my orthodontic care. I will have a beautiful set of straight teeth!

Postscript:

After getting braces, I met and later married the man of my dreams. Afterward, my husband shared that my confidence had initially attracted him. *What confirmation and irony!* At the time when I was most focused on doing right by myself, without concerns about others' perceptions of me, I was attracting that which I wholeheartedly desired. I learned a critical personal truth from this revelation: my life reflects my choices. *What I decide today, determines my tomorrow.*

Practice saying "I will...":

Think about recent situations when you yearned to say *"I will..."* but didn't. Why didn't you say *"I will..."*? What would you do differently if you had a do-over? Think forward to tomorrow and think of an ongoing situation in which you need to say *"I will..."* Take ten minutes, get in front of a mirror and practice saying *"I will..."* to yourself.

You can do it! Engage your will in standing up for yourself. Remember, your life reflects your choices. What you decide today, determines your tomorrow.

Every day, you make countless decisions that in their simplest forms are either moving you towards your goals or taking you away from them. Whether proactive or passive, these actions are decisive. Intentional by nature and training, I am an advocate of decisive action.

Regularly, I reaffirm my commitment to decisive action. As I think about where I am today, I realize it is the result of yesterday's decisions. Today, I'm an entrepreneur because of previous decisions. All those decisions took grit and pushed me well beyond my comfort zones. I had to embrace faith and dispel fear to make these decisions. A factor in embracing faith was my desire to be more.

My choices define my life. As shared earlier in my experience with braces, if my actions are causing consequences I don't like, I have the power to make different choices that provide desired results. I like being responsible for my choices. I set favorable conditions for attainment of my desired goals in saying to myself and others: *"I choose..."*, *"I am..."*, *"I believe in my dreams!"*, and *"I can...!"*

I CHOOSE...

Make and own your decisions. Everything starts with a decision. In Genesis, the Bible chronicles God's decision to create humankind in His image. God is spirit. So He created us to be spirit beings possessing creative speaking power like His.

God's first words to Adam and Eve were words of blessing, defining Adam's and Eve's purpose and declaring their dominion on earth. God empowered and expected them to reign. And they did – until relinquishing their authority to the enemy. Subsequently, Jesus came to earth to reclaim what was lost. With His resurrection, Jesus defeated and made an open show of the enemy; reclaimed the lost authority; and transferred it to Believers.

Our mandate from God to reign remains. He's equipped us to be overcomers. We are never underdogs.

Once I heard a reporter asking LeBron James about being an underdog. With much attitude, LeBron exclaimed, "I'm never an underdog!" His statement immediately clicked with me. I immediately thought, *"Yeah, I like that. I'm never an underdog!"*

I'm letting this mindset resonate within me. As a result, I have greater confidence and know I'm walking taller. I'm emboldened.

I recall seeing a former colleague in 2013. He didn't see or recognize me. I prepared to speak, but his appearance stopped me. Only his name tag on his uniform was familiar. He had aged profoundly since I had last seen him in 2009. Once energetic and lively, he now radiated stress and fatigue.

As I strolled past him, I reflected on our last conversation in 2009. He had boasted of his connections and certainty of promotion. Four years later, we were on different paths leading to our dream jobs. I had no regrets — I also had certainty of promotion. Why? Because I am an overcomer and I'm never an underdog!

I AM...

Proactively declare good things about yourself. Be your own cheerleader.

The Bible declares, "the tongue has the power of life and death..." (Proverbs 18:21). Using an agricultural analogy, this verse means words are like seeds. They are sown into the soil of hearers' hearts and they yield harvests.

Death-producing seeds are words that erode hearers' self-esteem. Conversely, life-producing seeds are words that affirm hearers' self-esteem. Seeds produce after their own kind. Accordingly, good seeds produce bountiful blooms.

In *The Power of I Am: Two Words That Will Change Your Life*, Joel Osteen shares the principle of "I am" in stating, " Whatever follows the "I am" will eventually find you...Whatever you follow the "I am" with, you're handing it an invitation, opening the door, and giving it permission to be in your life. The good news is you get to choose what follows the "I am."

I encourage you to choose "I am" beliefs that empower and move you towards your goals.

Earlier, I mentioned how empowered I felt by embracing the mindset of "I am never an underdog!" As I internalized this belief, I began to consider audacious, bigger dreams. I discerned God encouraging me to dream again. I incorporated this revelation in a portion of my Toastmaster Area's 2016 International Speech Presentation:

*Hi! I am **Dream Again!** Do you remember me? You and I used to be inseparable — doing the spectacular — letting our imaginations fly. Whatever it was, we didn't know the meaning of the word "impossible." We were best friends — hmm — a handshake of introduction seems awkward based on our past… sort of like needing caller ID to identify your mother's voice or as improbable as asking for permission to breathe.*

*What's up? We used to be tight, but life got in the way and you tasted failure. It tasted like burnt toast, bitter and dry, and you tossed the failure into your mind's trash bin. I understand your action but offer a counterintuitive response: **Dream Again!** Yes! **Dream Again!** Failure is a temporary event and valuable teacher – if you choose to learn from it.*

Sometimes failure simply tests your resolve. Consider this: an editor fired Walt Disney for being unimaginative.

Failure isn't final — unless you choose to let it be. How about flipping the script and seeing failure as proof of trying and risking? Please be advised, success has her own timeline. For example, Van Gogh painted more than 900 paintings and only sold one in his lifetime. Today, he's considered one of the greatest artists of all time.

I could go on and on, but it's unnecessary. I believe you got the message. I'll tell you a secret. I, **Dream Again**, am the flip side of failure. I, **Dream Again**, am your ally, and we can be inseparable again, disparaging thoughts of impossibility. You are equipped, have no doubt. This is your time; this is your life! I, **Dream Again**, am not a fantasy, I am your potential forecasting reality. Together, we will win, have no doubt. Destiny's calling, look within, and **Dream Again!**

The revelation of **Dream Again!** resonated deeply with the audience. In fact, the winner of the speech contest encouraged me to expand the reach of this revelation through writing about it. Hope surged within me at the thought of my message's relevance. That day in March 2016, I decided that somehow and some way I would share **Dream Again!** in my writing. How ironic that a speech contest would reinforce my dream and resolve to be a writer…

I BELIEVE IN MY DREAMS!

Know what matters to you. What societal issues move you to tears, joy, indignation, etc.? God created you to be a solution to some need in the world that matters to Him. In fact, your solutions to world needs are dreams that come from God. Your target may be as laser-focused as one person, as broad as the world, or somewhere in between. Your dreams matter.

I recall my sadness in reading Bruce Wilkinson's assessment of a young boy's death from starvation in *The Dream Giver: Following Your God-Given Destiny*. Bruce pondered why the child died. His conclusion was "I believe his Need was someone else's Dream — a Big and Important Dream that had not been embraced and pursued…Surely God placed a particular set of interests and abilities in one person…and put that person…where Great Things could happen — *should* have happened — for that boy."

Remember, God equipped you to succeed in addressing needs connected to your talents. Whatever your talents, no matter how insignificant they may appear to you, they are powerful.

The same God who gave you the dreams is well able to bring them to pass (Hebrews 10:23 and Romans 4:18-21). Especially when circumstances seem to be most bleak, choose to be like Abraham and entrust your dreams to God. Your dreams matter to God and God is faithful!

Knowing all things are possible with God (Matthew 19:26), a powerful response to our circumstances is "can do!" We can say this because God's Word in Philippians 4:13 reveals, "I can do all this through him who gives me strength."

I CAN…!

Inventory your strengths and talents and choose to use them as stepping stones to attaining your goals.

God has created you with talents that are solutions to others' needs. Burying your talents like the fearful steward in the parable of the talents will yield similar rebuke (Matthew 25:14-29). God expects us to gain increases on His investments in us. Importantly, our stewardship of His resources has temporal and eternal consequences.

If fear and/or self-limiting beliefs are keeping you from doing what you know you should do, I recommend you go straight to God's Word. His Word is the written record of His love for us. As we gain understanding and acceptance of His unlimited love for us, His love casts out fear. His Word has the healing virtue to restore us and uplift us to move out in faith.

God knows the good we are capable of. Let His love and support displace your fear. See Him in His Word, telling you, "Come" (Matthew 14:29). You can do what He has created you to do.

Practice saying *"I choose... I am... I believe in my dreams! and I can..."*

Choose to be more self-aware in your use of the phrases *"I choose..."*, *"I am..."*, *"I believe in my dreams!"*, and *"I can...!"* Learn and accept what God says about you. As you mix your faith with what He says about you and your circumstances, you can gain the confidence to proclaim:

1. *I choose...* (to eat healthy foods, drink water instead of soda, speak kindly, etc.)
2. *I am...* (talented, loved, capable, strong, successful, bold, youthful, proven, etc.)
3. *I can...* (learn, create, help, build, speak, etc.)

Use of these affirmative phrases will position you to more clearly see the possibility of your dreams. As you continue to focus on the positives of who you are and what you can do, you will find it easier to confidently say, *"I believe in my dreams!"*

Points to Remember

1. You have the power to choose what you believe about yourself.

2. Ever the bully, fear will taunt, strut, and denounce your efforts. Fear will also strive to get you to doubt God's love and good plans for you.

3. If you remain silent or agree with fear, you will reap a harvest of fear-dominated results; however, if you choose to respond with God's Word and dare to believe in the value of who you are and what you can do as God's child, you can defeat fear.

4. Victory begins in your mind. When you choose to face fear and act anyway, fear becomes a training ground, producing courage, experience, and testimonies. Continued decisive action will place your desired results within your grasp and fear beneath your feet.

5. Our mandate from God to reign remains. He's equipped us to be overcomers.

6. God created you to be a solution to some need in the world that matters to Him.

7. Whatever your talents, no matter how insignificant they may appear to you, they are powerful.

8. The same God who gave you the dreams is well able to bring them to pass (Hebrews 10:23 and Romans 4:18-21).

9. God knows the good we are capable of. Let His love and support displace your fear. See Him in His Word, telling you, "Come" (Matthew 14:29). You can do what He has created you to do.

PART THREE: BEHAVIORS

DREAM BIG!

Dreaming includes three critical actions:

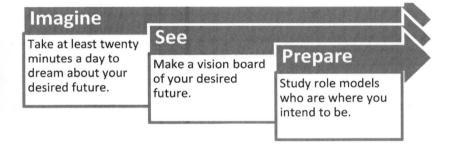

Imagine: Take at least twenty minutes a day to dream about your desired future.

See: Make a vision board of your desired future.

Prepare: Study role models who are where you intend to be.

Action Strategies:

- Be as specific as possible in visualizing your desired future. How does your desired future look, smell, feel, sound, etc.?

- Create a vision board, transforming your desired future to tangible pictures. Include power words in your vision board to create a "can do!" environment.

- Only consider attaining success…prepare for success, not failure! Believe that if you can dream it and see it, you can achieve it!

- Call those things that be not (Romans 4:17). In your inner dialogue, call yourself by the desired future titles, such as doctor, professor, chef, etc. Include these titles in your vision board.

- To know how your role models think, read and listen to their words. Use God's Word as the lens through which you analyze and embrace others' words.

Remember, the size of your dream should be based on God's ability — not yours — and be:

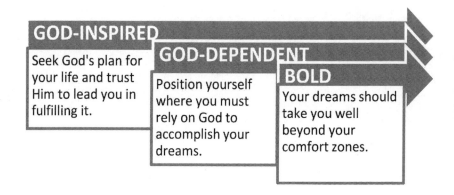

Action Strategies:

- Keep first things first. Seek God (Matthew 6:33) and listen for His direction before launching. Where He guides, He provides.
- If you can readily fulfill your dreams by your own efforts, your dreams are much smaller than God's dreams for you. Remember, God's dreams are based upon **His ability** and **your availability**.

- Increase your capacity to receive God's empowerment for your dreams.
- Learn something relevant to your desired future every day. Close each day wiser than you were when you awoke.
- Affirm the significance of your desired future every day. Loudly declare, "I matter! My talents are solutions to someone's problems."
- Encourage yourself by asserting, "I can do all this through him who gives me strength" (Philippians 4:13).

Have you ever dreamed a big dream, only to hear an internal voice shout, "You don't have what it takes!"? For me, small thinking is a bully. This bully appeals to my vulnerabilities and listening to small thinking is as invigorating as listening to elevator music.

If small thinking was a person, you could act to avoid or block it — like an unwanted phone call; instead, small thinking executes hostile takeovers in the decision-making conferences of your mind. It's an invader as unwanted as termites in a log cabin. I so strongly believe in big thinking that I created a farewell to small thinking. Years ago, I remember hearing there are two basic kinds of military farewells. One is a farewell in which you hate to see the honoree leave and the other is one in which you attend just to make sure the honoree is really leaving. Today's occasion is the latter:

Today, I refuse to enable small thinking to rob me. I know faith and fear can't occupy the same space. The same is true for big and small thinking. I choose big thinking! Small thinking, you're evicted, now!

Small thinking, I do not wish you well. May you forever flee from the power of a believing heart. Don't even think about returning to my being. You aren't welcome in my thoughts, words, and actions! Be gone!

PLAN HOW YOU CAN

My action plan for getting from where I am to my desired destination has 5 steps:

The five steps are straightforward:

1. Identify your desired destination.
2. Determine your start point.
3. Determine the steps needed to move from your start point to your desired destination. Importantly, the sum of steps will create a path leading to your desired destination.
4. Get and stay on the path with daily decisive action. Don't quit!

5. Follow the path to its end, which will be your desired destination.

Daily action is such a pivotal step, it bears further explanation. The two reinforcing actions for daily action are "Show Up!" and "Take Your Place!"

SHOW UP!

If I want to be a college graduate, it only makes sense that I show up for my college classes and complete the specified requirements. Absence and incompletion of requirements are steps on the path of failure, regardless of intentions.

Success begins with getting (or showing up) on the path leading to your desired destination. Advancement along the path requires demonstration of the qualities needed for thriving at the desired destination. For example, can you think of a world champion who is undisciplined in mastering his/her craft? If so, I question how long the person will remain a world champion. In fact, I agree with Alan Armstrong's assertion that "champions do not become champions when they win the event, but in the hours, weeks, months, and years they spend preparing for it. The victorious performance itself is merely the demonstration of their championship character."

Staying on the path to your desired destination is challenging. Discipline must displace excuses and procrastination. Discipline, the consistent act of doing what you know to be right, is a compass to staying on the path. A mindset of discipline enables you to "Take Your Place!"

TAKE YOUR PLACE!

I believe "Take Your Place!" asserts:

- You operate from a mindset of abundance.
- You take personal leadership for who you are, where you are, and what you want.
- Your skills, experiences, and values can secure places for you.

I appreciate roadmaps. The roadmap I use for *"Take Your Place!"* is the Army's leadership "Be, Know, Do" model, significantly modified for my purposes:

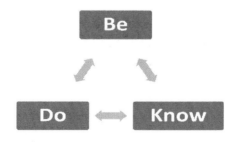

I'll use the context of job hunting to explain my use of the modified "Be, Know, Do" model:

Be: Be the best representation and reconciliation of self and your desired destination in how you show up in person and electronically.

- Resume: Do the words of your resume reflect who you are and aspire to be?
- LinkedIn profile: Do the profile materials clearly speak to who you are and aspire to be?
- Physical Presence: Do your demeanor, attire, and communication reflect who you are and desire to be?
- Online Presence: Does your online presence align with the values and activities upheld by your desired hiring organizations?

Know: Know how to identify, apply, and evaluate the degree of fit between yourself and your desired destination.

- How does your conversation reflect your knowledge and skill sets?
- How aware are you of your readiness for your desired destination?
- How are you uniquely equipped for this desired destination?
- What value do you provide to your desired destination?

Do: Take actions that declare fitness for your desired destination.

- What are your associations with the desired destination?
- How visible are your actions in attaining your desired destination?
- How consistent are your actions in attaining your desired destination?
- How consistent are your actions in preparing to thrive in your desired destination?

For illustration of this concept, I'll use food service metaphors and contexts to reinforce understanding:

- If you are spinach applying to a donut shop, expect low to no interest.
- If you're tofu applying to a burger restaurant, you've got some heavy persuading ahead of you.

It is so important for you to fulfill your life purposes! You can get to your desired destination! Truly, I understand how the thought of staying on a path for months and years could seem intimidating. Instead of focusing on the months and years, I choose to focus on a much smaller period. I focus on one day — **today** — the only day I have.

Knowing that "Life happens," my focus on just one day, today, is forgiving. Each new day provides a new opportunity to start over with resolve and expectation. If I have a tough day and don't meet my daily action plan goals, I assess what happened, determine a strategy to do better the next day, and commit to do better the next day.

Any failures experienced are seen as separate events, not states of being (*translation: I may have failed a task, but I am not a failure!*). Failures are also opportunities to learn how to better lead myself.

With this daily focus, any needed corrections should be minimal, helping me to stay on the path to my desired destination. Empowerment flows from knowing God provides us new mercies each day (Lamentations 3:23) and the Lord's Prayer (Matthew 6:9-13) in which we ask for daily bread.

In short, the daily focus is intended to empower, not condemn. If you commit to this daily focus and treat yourself lovingly *while* holding yourself accountable, you will succeed if you don't quit.

In the morning, I tell myself that whatever good I do that day will be enough. In the evening, I applaud what I've accomplished. These bookends of affirmation support my decision to do *all I can each day to reach my desired future – one step at a time!*

Know this: **You can do it! You matter.** *You are designed to succeed at being you!*

When, *not if,* you face resistance and are pressured to quit, I urge you to keep your dreams. I speak what I know and believe. In my Toastmaster Area's 2018 International Speech Contest Presentation, I shared early experiences in keeping my dreams:

Anyone familiar with the tv show called Let's Make A Deal? In life, we face the same **QUESTION: Do you want to make a deal?**

I recall Monty Roberts' experience of being the son of a poor horse trainer. As a high school senior, Monty wrote a seven-page paper describing his goal of owning a horse ranch. His teacher gave him an F and said, "There's no way you could ever do it…if you will rewrite this paper with a more realistic goal, I will reconsider your grade." **TRANSLATION: Do you want to make a deal?**

*Monty kept his paper for a week and then turned it in with no changes. He told his teacher, "You can keep the F and I'll keep my dream." I've faced similar pressures to trade my dreams for something less. Around kindergarten (yes, that early in life), I was subjected to aptitude testing without my mother's consent. Test results showed I should pursue a vocational track and I would be lucky **if** I graduated high school. Here it comes -* **QUESTION: Do you want to make a deal?**

My mother had the option of choosing the test results held in my teachers' hands or visions of my potential held in her heart. From my kindergarten through fifth grade years, she fought teacher expectations and I focused on doing my best work. By the sixth grade, the child who had sat at the back of the class was now sitting in the front row. Six years later, I graduated high school as valedictorian of my class.

If someone or something has tried to talk you into trading your dreams for something less, you can assert your power and just say "No!"

Yes, I advise you to tell life, "Thanks for the choice. I'll take what's in my heart. **I'll keep my dreams!***"*

TAKE A STEP FORWARD EVERY DAY!

I'm intrigued there are 86,400 seconds in a day. I've also wondered who thinks of a day in terms of seconds? I think of a day in terms of minutes and have recently adopted the twenty-minute action block. During the twenty-minute action block, I give the task at hand my full attention. If the task requires more than twenty minutes, I determine how many more twenty-minute blocks I'll allocate to completion or getting to a stop point.

To ensure I'm investing my time in efforts that most matter to me, I have also learned to structure my daily work according to the rule of three:

1. I pursue only a maximum of three goals at a time.

2. Each day, I strive to whole-heartedly complete only three "to do" action items, which are related to my three goals. I keep things simple and maintain my focus. This strategy guides me in knowing what to do *and* what not to do.

Here's my daily action plan template:

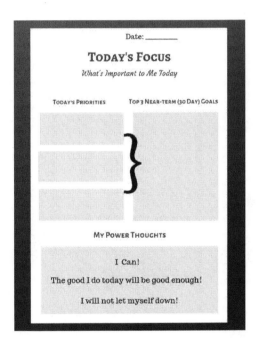

Though the action plan template is straightforward, I will further explain its priorities and near-term goals sections:

- **Today's Priorities:** Enables listing of three priorities for the day. These priorities flow from the three near-term goals. Your daily actions need to take you closer, each day, to your desired destination. The small number of priorities helps you to stay focused and make meaningful progress on what matters most to you.

- **Top Three Near-Term (30 Day) Goals**: These goals are the basic steps leading to fulfillment of longer-range goals. In fulfilling the near-term goals, you build a record of accomplishment and completion that keeps you on path to ultimately reach your desired destination.

Using the context of a rising high school senior, a sample action plan could look like:

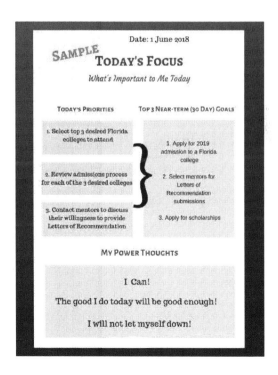

Looking at the sample action plan, the rising senior has three actions planned that are supportive of two of her three near-term goals. By day's end, she'll understand the admission processes for her top three desired colleges and will have made contacts with mentors to discuss their willingness to submit letters of recommendation.

On a different day, she can focus on actions related to her near-term goal of applying for scholarships. As these near-term goals are met, she can progress to other near-term goals that will take her closer toward her long-term goal of college admission in 2019.

The daily focus keeps her proactive and able to maximize opportunities available to early applicants for admission and scholarships.

I am such a fan of the daily focus because it gives me daily proof that I'm moving closer towards who I desire to become. The consistency of my actions produces power, which expands my capacity to tackle other actions. I have used this approach since 2016 and it has empowered me to produce multiple written works and oversee two college scholarship programs while executing two family moves.

CLOSING

You will have times when you'll have to encourage yourself. During a rough spot in 2016, I chose to forgo a pity party for one and penned the following:

I Will, I Am

Attitude is critical.

How I interpret my circumstances establishes their outcome.

Victor or victim, it's really my call.

I can't control other's actions, but I can control my response.

If I fall or get pushed down, whether I stay down depends on me. It's my call.

Yesterday, I learned there are 86,400 seconds in a day – with no carryover!

Yesterday, I realized time is one resource I can't hoard.

Yesterday, I questioned who I'd be.

Yesterday, I realized each day's decisions form who I'll be.

Yesterday, I said I wanted to be a writer. So, I wrote a book and launched it, hands shaking, on Amazon.

Today, I saw my first book on Amazon and chose an unapologetic writer I'd be.

Today, I decided not to quit.

Today, I willed myself to do what writers do. **I will** write for **I am** a writer!

Tomorrow, **I will** write for **I am** a writer.

The poem worked. I felt encouraged to keep my commitment to writing. What about you? What words speak to you when you need encouragement?

I know a place you can go to that will never fail – no matter the situation or time of day. You're always welcome and have no charge to pay. Whatever your issue, have no fear — the Source of your counsel has seen and conquered it all.

What's this Source? The Living Word of God!

God and His Word are one. My "go to" power Scriptures include:

- Psalm 5:12 – "Surely, LORD, you bless the righteous; you surround them with Your favor as with a shield."
- Psalm 23:1 – "The LORD is my shepherd, I lack nothing."
- Psalm 37:4 – "Take delight in the LORD, and he will give you the desires of your heart."
- Psalm 91:14-16 – "Because he loves me," says the LORD, "I will rescue him; I will protect him, for he acknowledges my name. He will call on me, and I will answer him; I will be with him in trouble, I will deliver him and honor him. With long life I will satisfy him and show him my salvation."
- Ephesians 2:10 – "For we are God's handiwork, created in Christ Jesus to do good works, which God prepared in advance for us to do."
- Isaiah 43:1-2 – "Do not fear, for I have redeemed you; I have summoned you by name; you are mine. When you pass through the waters, I will be with you; and when you pass through the rivers, they will not sweep over you. When you walk through the fire, you will not be burned; the flames will not set you ablaze."
- Jeremiah 1:5 – "Before I formed you in the womb, I knew you…"
- Jeremiah 31:3 – "I have loved you with an everlasting love; I have drawn you with unfailing kindness."
- Luke 1:37 – "For no word from God will ever fail."

- John 3:16 – "For God so loved the world that He gave His one and only Son, that whoever believes in him shall not perish but have eternal life."
- Romans 8:37-39 – "No, in all these things we are more than conquerors through him who loved us. For I am convinced that neither death nor life, neither angels nor demons, neither the present nor the future, nor any powers, neither height nor depth, nor anything else in all creation, will be able to separate us from the love of God that is in Christ Jesus our Lord."
- Philippians 4:6-7 – "Do not be anxious about anything, but in every situation, by prayer and petition, with thanksgiving, present your requests to God. And the peace of God, which transcends all understanding, will guard your hearts and minds in Christ Jesus."
- Philippians 4:13 – "I can do all this through him who gives me strength."
- 2 Timothy 1:7 – "For the Spirit God gave us does not make us timid, but gives us power, love, and self-discipline."

I could go on, but you get the idea. I encourage you to develop your own "go to" Scripture list that empowers you to pursue and attain your goals. Be sure to mix these Scriptures with your faith as you *speak them out loud, often, and in the face of fear*. Yes, as you **speak God's Word over fear**, you position yourself for success. Remember, you haven't been given the spirit of fear, but of "power, love, and self-discipline" (2 Timothy 1:7).

God calls His children more than conquerors (Romans 8:37) and overcomers (1 John 4:4 and 1 John 5:4-5). Fear belongs beneath your feet.

You are designed to succeed at being you. Go forth and ***Speak Over the Fear!***

ABOUT THE AUTHOR

CEO of *Intentionally Me*, an innovative leadership and professional development company, Dr. Stephanie L. Foster provides a nurturing place for others to recognize, develop, and use their talents to fulfill their life purposes. In this book, she has shared what she knows to be true: You are designed to succeed at being you.

Other books by Dr. Stephanie L. Foster:

- Talking Myself Into My Desired Future: God's Way
- Me, Intentionally: 7 Biblical Strategies for Godly Success

Please visit www.intentionallymellc.com to either learn more about *Intentionally Me* or to submit a speaking request.

REFERENCES

Headquarters, Department of the Army (1999). *Army Leadership* (FM 22-100). Retrieved from www.armyheritage.org/images/Education/FMs/FM%2022-100%20Aug99.pdf.

Osteen, Joel. *The Power of I Am*. Hachette Book Group, 2015, pp. 1-2.

Wilkinson, Bruce and David and Heather Kopp. *The Dream Giver*. Multnomah Books, 2003, pp. 142, 147.

Manufactured by Amazon.ca
Bolton, ON